(4)

To Joyce
All good wishes
Cynthia Venn.

SMOCKING IN SUGARPASTE

CYNTHIA VENN

MEREHURST
LONDON

DEDICATION

Thanks to my husband, Rob, who has helped me so much with this book, also to the rest of my family and friends for their continued interest.

A special 'thank you' is due to Sally for helping me to conquer the 'demon' word processor.

NOTES ON USING THE RECIPES

For all recipes, quantities are given in metric,
Imperial and cups. Follow one set of measures only
as they are not interchangeable.

All spoon measures refer to a standard set of measuring spoons
and they are always level unless otherwise stated.
1 teaspoon = 5 ml
1 tablespoon = 15 ml

Eggs used in the recipes are standard size 3
unless otherwise stated.

Ovens should be pre-heated to the specified temperature.

CONTENTS

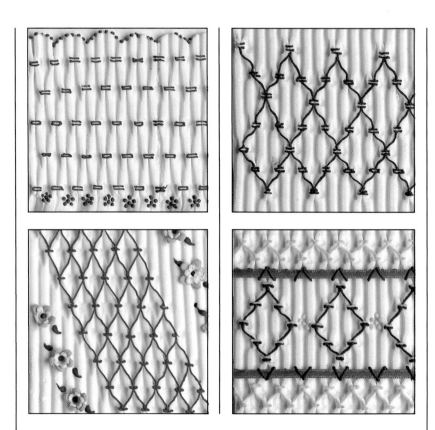

Clockwise from top left:
Honeycomb stitch panel. Scalloped edge with piped dots.
Piped flower border above frilled edge.

Large diamond design. First row: alternate pairs of ridges
pinched. Second row: every pair pinched. Third row: ridges
left free in first row are pinched. Repeated in reverse.

Diamond design with honeycomb stitch borders, over-piped
ribbon and tiny piped flowers.

Diagonal band of surface honeycomb stitch. Each row is
started one ridge to the right. The same number of ridges
are pinched in each row.

INTRODUCTION

The art of smocking is said to have evolved from the Anglo Saxon 'smocc' which resembled the chemise or the shirt.

The original smocks were cut along simple lines and made entirely of rectangular pieces of material which were embroidered over pleats in the bodice and sleeves. The smocking was functional: it held the garment in to the shape of the body and its elasticity made the garment very comfortable to wear.

Peasants who worked on the land wore simple, full, knee-length smocks over their other clothes to keep them clean as well as for protection against the wind and rain. The superior status of English countrymen was reflected by their 'Sunday-best' smocks which were richly embroidered. These decorative garments were highly prized within families and they were handed down from one generation to the next as their owners died.

The smock began to disappear from the countryside at the time of the industrial revolution. The introduction of mechanised farm machinery meant that these flowing garments represented a safety hazard and they were replaced by more practical tighter-fitting clothing. Luckily the style was preserved by fashion-conscious ladies of the late nineteenth century when smocked ladies and children's dresses became a speciality of several London dressmakers.

Now, in the late twentieth century, we are experiencing a revival of interest in smocking with the emphasis on its decorative qualities. As a decorative art, smocking readily adapts to a variety of uses for home decorations and gifts as well as for making clothes look more attractive.

One of the most creative ways in which the potential of smocking has developed is in the art of cake decorating. Traditional smocking stitches may be adapted to open up endless possibilities for sugarcraft designs, some of which are featured in this book. I have developed all the techniques, and the smocking equipment used in this book, and I hope this introduction to sugarpaste smocking will inspire you, the reader, to experiment with new designs to delight us all.

EQUIPMENT

Apart from the usual equipment required for preparing sugarpaste and covering cakes, there are two key items used for the smocking technique. A special grooved roller has been carefully designed to produce authentic-looking smocking. The ridges on the roller are exactly the same distance apart as they are deep and they will form the perfect base for the smocking. The ridges are manufactured to the correct gauge to be in proportion to an average-sized cake. The roller will make 15cm (6 in) wide pieces of smocking. It is neither practical nor desirable to make wider strips of smocking as a certain amount of stretching would occur when lifting them and the line of the pattern would be altered. It is very easy to make an invisible join between panels of smocking by butting the pieces against each other: the seam is lost between the ridges.

The second, small piece of essential equipment is the pair of tweezers. These are designed for setting the shape produced by stitching in traditional smocking, by carefully pinching together the 'pleats' that are made with the roller. The roller is neat enough to fit into even the smallest work box and the tweezers can be safely stowed away in the roller's hollow centre.

EQUIPMENT FOR SMOCKING IN SUGARPASTE

Around the outside, clockwise from top left:
cake boards and nylon sieve
thick foam
fine ribbons
food colouring
cutters: three sizes of ivy leaf cutter, broderie anglais cutter, circular garrett frill cutter and carnation cutter
small scissors
cocktail sticks (toothpicks)
scriber
fine paint brush
scalpel

artist's cranked palette knife
straight scalloped cutter
modelling tools
Easter egg moulds
greaseproof paper
large, straight-edged kitchen knife

In the middle, from the top:
smoothers
icing tubes (tips), greaseproof paper
icing bag and fine brush for cleaning tubes (tips)
smocking equipment: plastic tweezers and ridged roller
plain white plastic rolling pin

BASIC RECIPES

SUGARPASTE

Also known as rolled fondant. This recipe uses the cold method to make fondant for rolling out.

5 teaspoons powdered gelatine
50ml (2 fl oz/¼ cup) cold water
25g (1 oz/1 tablespoon) glycerine
125ml (4 fl oz/½ cup) liquid glucose
900g (1 lb 13 oz/5½ cups) icing (confectioner's) sugar, sifted

Sprinkle the gelatine over the cold water in a small bowl. Leave to soften for 2–3 minutes, until sponged. Place in a saucepan of hot water and stir until dissolved. Do not boil the water under the gelatine. Add glycerine and glucose to the gelatine, then stir until both have melted.

Place the sifted icing sugar in a large bowl. Make a well in the sugar and add the gelatine mixture. Mix the ingredients with a palette knife at first, then knead to a soft, smooth consistency. Makes about 1kg (2 lb).

ROYAL ICING

75ml (3 fl oz/generous ⅓ cup) egg whites or 75ml (3 fl oz/generous ⅓ cup) cold water mixed with 15g (½ oz/3 teaspoons) powdered albumen
500g (1 lb/3 cups) icing (confectioner's) sugar, sifted

Strain egg whites or albumen into a grease-free bowl. Add the sifted icing sugar and beat on the slowest speed of a heavy-duty electric mixer for 10 minutes. Place in an airtight container, then allow the icing to rest overnight. Stir the icing by hand before using.

Alternatively, the icing may be mixed by hand. Add half the sugar to the egg white. Beat well by hand for about 10 minutes, until smooth and thoroughly combined. Add the rest of the sugar gradually mixing well between each addition.

Note For perfect results, the volume of egg white used to make royal icing should be measured. About 3 egg whites will give 75ml (3 fl oz/ generous ⅓ cup).

MODELLING PASTE

Modelling paste keeps well for several weeks. Store it in a thick polythene bag (use a spotlessly clean, new bag) in an airtight container. Do not put the modelling paste in the refrigerator.

4 teaspoons powdered gelatine
50ml (2 fl oz/¼ cup) cold water
2 teaspoons liquid glucose
450g (14½ oz/2¾ cups) icing (confectioner's) sugar, sifted

Sprinkle gelatine over the water in a small bowl. Leave to soften for 2–3 minutes, until sponged. Place in a saucepan of hot water and stir until dissolved. Do not boil the water under the gelatine. Add glucose to gelatine, then stir until melted.

Place the sifted icing sugar in a large bowl. Make a well in the sugar and add the gelatine mixture. Stir with palette knife until well mixed, then knead until smooth and pliable. Place the paste in a polythene bag and leave for several hours before using. Makes about 500g (1 lb).

SMOCKING PASTE

The reason for adding gum tragacanth or gum paste to sugarpaste is to make it strong enough to hold the pattern of the smocking while still remaining soft for cutting.

white vegetable fat
½ teaspoon gum tragacanth
500g (1 lb) sugarpaste (rolled fondant), opposite

Coat your hands well with white vegetable fat. Knead the powdered gum tragacanth into the sugarpaste until throughly combined. Place in a clean polythene bag and allow to rest for several hours before using. Makes about 500g (1 lb).

Note Alternatively, make smocking paste using 500g (1 lb) sugarpaste (rolled fondant) kneaded with 125g (4oz/¼ lb) any flower modelling paste which contains gum tragacanth. This paste does not have to stand, it may be used immediately.

GELATINE PASTE

Gelatine paste may be used instead of modelling paste for making boxes, bells, cards and other shaped items. This paste is very strong and it is quick to make but it has a short working life as it will set within 30 minutes of being made. All equipment should be assembled before making the paste.

1 teaspoon powdered gelatine
3 tablespoons cold water
500g (1 lb/3 cups) icing (confectioner's) sugar

Sprinkle gelatine over the water in a small bowl. Leave to soften for 2–3 minutes, until sponged. Place in a saucepan of hot water and stir until dissolved. Do not boil the water under the gelatine. Remove from heat.

Sift the icing sugar onto a clean dry surface. Take about 1 tablespoon of sugar from the sifted icing sugar and stir it rapidly into the gelatine mixture with a wooden spoon. Continue adding sugar by the table-spoonful, rapidly stirring in each addition, until the mixture is the consistency of thick cream.

Make a well in the remaining sugar. Pour the gelatine mixture into the centre and gradually mix the ingredients. Knead until the sugar is thoroughly combined and the paste no longer feels sticky. The strong paste is now ready for shaping ornaments. Store the paste in a strong polythene bag and remove all the air. Work with small pieces at a time as leftovers will not be suitable for re-use. Makes about 500g (1 lb).

RICH FRUIT CAKE

These quantities make a 20cm (8 in) round cake. When adjusting the mixture to make cakes of other sizes, the ingredients should be increased or decreased in the same proportions.

450g (14½ oz/2½ cups) sultanas (white raisins)
350g (11 oz/2 cups) raisins
225g (7 oz/1½ cups) currants
100g (3½ oz/½ cup) glacé cherries
65g (2 oz/⅓ cup) citrus peel, chopped
65g (2 oz/½ cup) blanched almonds, slivered
grated rind and juice of 1 lemon
3 tablespoons brandy
250g (8 oz/1 cup) butter or margarine
250g (8 oz/1½ cups) soft brown sugar
4 eggs, at room temperature
250g (8 oz/2 cups) plain (all purpose) flour
½ teaspoon ground mixed spice

Mix all the fruit and nuts in a large mixing bowl with the lemon rind and juice. Stir in the brandy, cover and leave to soak for several hours or overnight.

Grease a 20cm (8 in) round cake tin and line with greaseproof paper. Grease the paper well. Pre-heat the oven to 150°C (300°F/Gas 2). Cream butter or magarine and sugar until light and fluffy. Beat the eggs and add to the butter mixture a little at a time, beating thoroughly between each addition. If the mixture begins to curdle, add a spoonful of the flour at this stage.

Sift the flour and spice together and add to the mixture, stirring thoroughly until smooth and well combined. Add the soaked fruit with all its juices and stir in thoroughly. Turn the mixture into the prepared tin, smooth it down and level off the top.

Bake the cake for 3½–3¾ hours. To check if the cake is cooked, insert a clean skewer into the centre. If it comes out clean the cake is cooked; if there are any signs of sticky mixture on the skewer, then continue to cook and test the cake after another 15 minutes. Another test is to check that the mixture has stopped sizzling: it becomes quiet when it is cooked, if the cake is still making sizzling noises, then continue to cook. Leave the cake in the tin until it is cold.

ALMOND PASTE

Raw eggs are used in this almond paste. They should be perfectly fresh and obtained from a reputable source. If you have any doubts about the quality of the eggs, or if there is any danger that they may contain salmonella bacteria, this recipe should not be used. Commercial marzipan is made from sterilized egg products and it may be used quite safely.

125g (4 oz/³⁄₄ cup) icing (confectioner's) sugar, sifted
125g (4 oz/¹⁄₂ cup) caster (superfine) sugar
225g (7 oz/2 cups) ground almonds
1 teaspoon lemon juice
almond or vanilla essence (flavoring), to taste
1 whole egg or 2 yolks, beaten

Mix the icing and caster sugars with the ground almonds in a bowl. Make well in the centre, then add lemon juice, a drop of the chosen essence and a little beaten egg. Mix the ingredients adding sufficient egg to make a firm but malleable dough.

Turn the dough on to a work surface lightly dusted with icing sugar and knead until firm. Do not over-knead as this will release too much oil from the almonds and the dough will become greasy. Wrap in plastic wrap or foil until required. Makes about 500g (1 lb).

Note Where recipes refer to marzipan, use the above recipe or the commercial product.

A GUIDE TO QUANTITIES OF MARZIPAN AND SUGARPASTE FOR COVERING CAKES

In the case of a heavy fruit cake the quantity of marzipan or sugarpaste (rolled fondant) may be calculated by weighing the cake. Halve the weight of the cake to give the amount of marzipan or sugarpaste needed for covering the top and sides of the cake. For example a cake which weighs 1kg (2 lb) in total will require 500g (1 lb) marzipan or sugarpaste to cover both the top and sides.

Alternatively, the quantity of marzipan or sugarpaste may be calculated according to the size of the cake. This method should be used for Madeira cakes. The following quantities will be sufficient for either a heavy fruit cake or a lighter Madeira cake. The sizes and quantities are an average for both round and square cakes. The smallest and largest cakes will use slightly less marzipan or sugarpaste if they are round, and slightly more if they are square.

Cake Size	Weight of Marzipan or Sugarpaste
15cm (6 in)	500g (1 lb)
18cm (7 in)	625g (1¼ lb)
20cm (8 in)	750g (1½ lb)
23cm (9 in)	875g (1¾ lb)
25cm (10 in)	1kg (2 lb)
28cm (11 in)	1.25kg (2½ lb)
30cm (12 in)	1.5kg (3 lb)

Madeira Cake

This recipe may be used as an alternative to rich fruit cake. It is firm enough to make a good base for decorating. To avoid the mixture curdling, all the ingredients should be at room temperature. These quantities make one 20cm (8 in) round cake or an 18cm (7 in) square cake. When adjusting the mixture to make cakes of other sizes, the ingredients should be increased or decreased in the same proportions.

175g (6 oz/¾ cup) butter
175g (6 oz/¾ cup) caster (superfine) sugar
3 eggs, beaten
125g (4 oz/1 cup) self-raising (self-rising) flour
50g (1½ oz/½ cup) plain (all purpose) flour
50g (1½ oz/½ cup) ground almonds
grated rind of 1 orange
about 2 tablespoons orange juice

Preheat the oven to 180°C (350°F/Gas 4). Grease a 20cm (8 in) round or 18cm (7 in) square cake tin and line with greaseproof paper. Grease the paper well. Cream butter and sugar until light and fluffy. Add the beaten eggs a little at a time, beating thoroughly between each addition.

Sift the self-raising and plain flours with ground almonds. Fold the dry ingredients into the creamed mixture with the orange rind. Add enough orange juice to make a soft dropping consistency. Turn the mixture into the prepared tin, smooth it down and level off the top. Bake the cake for 1–1¼ hours.

To check if the cake is cooked, insert a clean skewer into the centre. If it comes out clean, the cake is cooked; if there are any signs of sticky mixture on the skewer, then continue to cook and test the cake after another 10 minutes. Leave the cake to cool in the tin for a few minutes, then turn it out onto a wire cooling rack.

SMOCKING TECHNIQUES

Smocking is a form of embroidery which is worked on the surface of material which has previously been gathered into tiny pleats. This distinguishes it from other types of embroidery. When applied to clothing smocking serves the dual purpose of holding in the fullness of material to fit the body and decorating the garment.

Sugarpaste smocking is purely decorative and it is intended to represent the effect of neat pleats of material decorated with embroidery. All the stitch designs used for sugarpaste work are based on authentic smocking.

The stitches fall into two main groups: straight stitches and zig zag stitches. The straight stitches are used mostly for borders and they do not affect the line of the pleats. Zig zag stitches are worked to distort the pleating, so creating a particular style of smocking.

The piped embroidery 'stitches' worked on sugarpaste cannot distort the pleats in the same way as sewing threads which are used to pull the folds of material into the traditional designs. To achieve this effect in sugarpaste, special tweezers provided in a smocking kit are used to set the designs before piping on the embroidery stitches in icing. The following illustrations clearly distinguish the different stitches that are used throughout the book. Detailed step-by-step instructions for setting the pattern follow on pages 18–21.

DIFFERENT SMOCKING STITCHES

These illustrations (right) show exactly how the pattern for the piped stitches should be set using the tweezers. The tweezers are used to pinch together the pleats of sugarpaste at the points where stitches are to be piped in icing. The photographs on page 4 highlight finished panels of the sugarpaste smocking.

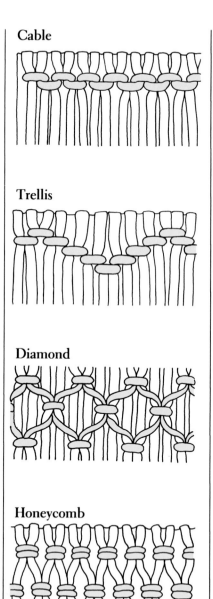

Cable

Trellis

Diamond

Honeycomb

Surface Honeycomb or Chevron

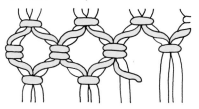

Double Cable

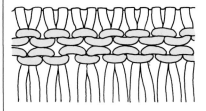

Wave

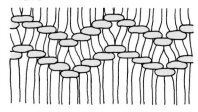

INGREDIENTS AND EQUIPMENT FOR COVERING AND DECORATING CAKES

rich fruit cake or Madeira cake, see pages 11 and 13
marzipan, see page 12, optional
sugarpaste (rolled fondant), see pages 8 and 12
smocking paste, see page 9
icing (confectioner's) sugar for rolling out
alcohol, for example vodka, gin or other spirit,
or apricot jam, boiled and sieved
royal icing, see page 8
food colouring

Equipment

smocking equipment
icing tubes (tips)

A rich fruit cake is usually covered with marzipan or almond paste before the sugarpaste is applied. The marzipan adds to the flavour but its most important role is to prevent the dark cake from discolouring the pale icing. A better surface on the finished icing also results from having a good foundation of marzipan. If you do not want to cover the cake with marzipan, mould a thin coating of sugarpaste around the cake and allow it to set before applying the top coat of sugarpaste.

A plain cake of the Madeira type does not need marzipan and the sugarpaste may be applied directly to the cake. The cake should be brushed with boiled, sieved apricot jam. For a perfect finish you will need to apply two layers of sugarpaste.

COVERING A CAKE WITH SUGARPASTE

You will need sufficient sugarpaste to cover the cake, see page 12. Rings will cause marks in the paste and should be removed from the fingers if possible. Roll out the sugarpaste on sifted icing (confectioner's) sugar. The paste should be about 5mm (¼ in) thick. If the cake is coated with marzipan, moisten it by brushing all over with a spirit such as gin or vodka. If the paste is going directly on the cake, brush the cake all over with boiled, sieved apricot jam. Lift the sugarpaste carefully by draping it over a rolling pin, and lay it centrally over the cake. With perfectly clean hands mould the paste to the shape of the cake, smoothing out any wrinkles and pricking any bubbles with a pin to release the air. Trim excess paste from around the base of the cake. Small holes and creases may be removed by rubbing the paste gently with the index finger, working in small circular movements. Use plastic smoothers to improve the finish of the paste.

Covering a Board and Cake with Sugarpaste

1 Begin by covering the board. Smooth rolled-out sugarpaste evenly over the board and trim the edges neatly. Leave to harden before covering the cake and putting it on the board.

5 Mould the paste to the shape of the cake, gently easing in fullness to avoid folds and creases.

2 Roll out the sugarpaste for covering the cake on a clean surface which is lightly sifted with icing (confectioner's) sugar. The paste should be about 5mm (¼ in) thick.

3 Lightly brush the marzipan-covered cake all over with alcohol.

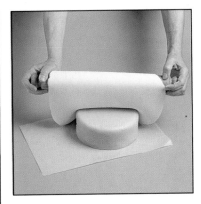

4 Lift the paste by draping it over a rolling pin. Place it centrally over the cake.

6 Trim off excess paste from around the base of the cake.

7 Smooth the paste to remove any small holes and tiny creases. Use a clean pin to prick any small air bubbles.

8 Gently lift the cake into position on the board. Use smoothers to lift the cake and avoid finger marks. Smooth out any small blemishes. The finished covering of sugarpaste should be even and completely smooth.

PLANNING AND SETTING THE SMOCKING

Plan the overall design of the cake and decide how the smocking is to be incorporated into the design before you begin working on the smocking panels. Make a paper template to fit the sides of the cake and use it as a guide to ensure that the pattern is evenly spaced. For a round, heart-shaped, or oval cake, cut a strip of paper the same depth as the cake and the same length as the circumference of the cake. For a square, hexagonal, or octagonal cake, cut a template of one side of the cake only. Mark the chosen design on the template and place it around the cake. Transfer the design to the surface of the cake by pricking through the template with a fine, clean pin.

Using the illustrations of stitches shown on pages 14–15 as a guide, practise a few of the designs before attempting to apply them to the cake. Dust a clean non-stick surface with cornflour (cornstarch) or icing (confectioner's) sugar. With a plain rolling pin, roll out smocking paste slightly larger than the width required and approximately 3mm (⅛ in) thick. The maximum width of the paste must not be larger than the length of the special ribbed roller. Using the ribbed roller, roll the paste firmly from bottom to top. Using a large knife to avoid dragging the paste, trim the side edges straight. Cut the top and bottom edges to the exact depth required: use a cardboard template cut 1cm (½ in) shorter than the depth of the cake.

Following the stitch guide, set the chosen pattern in the trimmed paste. To do this, gently squeeze pairs of ridges together, coaxing them out of their straight lines and into the required pattern. Continue with this technique until the completed pattern has been worked on the strip of sugarpaste.

APPLYING THE PANEL TO THE CAKE

Moisten the corresponding area of the cake by brushing lightly with alcohol. Carefully slide a palette knife under the panel of smocking, then lift it evenly and use your fingers to gently press it into position against the cake. Take care not to stretch the paste or distort the pattern. Continue until the required number of strips or panels have been applied to the cake. When a series of panels are applied to a cake to create a band of smocking, it is vital that the last panel to be added exactly fits the space left on the cake.

Important Points to Remember

1 Always make sure there is a little cornflour (cornstarch) on the surface under the paste to prevent it sticking as you work.

2 Roll the grooves firmly and evenly to obtain a well-defined pattern.

3 When using the tweezers to set the pattern, use even pressure with the thumb and finger.

4 In humid conditions the paste may feel a little sticky. To prevent the grooved roller from sticking, rub a little cornflour (cornstarch) over the surface of the paste before rolling.

Planning and Setting the Smocking

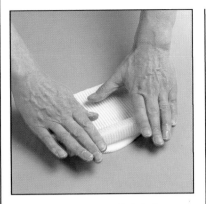

1 Roll out the paste slightly larger than the required width and approximately 3mm (⅛ in) thick. Using the special grooved roller, roll the paste from bottom to top.

2 Trim the side edges with a large knife.

3 Using a cardboard template, cut the paste to 1cm (½ in) shorter than the depth of the cake. Trim the top and bottom edges.

4 Instead of using a knife, the edges may be trimmed with a straight scalloped cutter.

5 Using the tweezers, set the pattern by gently squeezing together pairs of ridges.

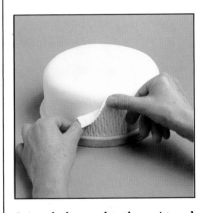

6 Attach the panel to the moistened cake.

PIPING THE EMBROIDERY

The embroidery is always piped directly onto the cake. The cake should be placed on a turntable which should slightly tilt away from you. Use fresh royal icing, see page 8, and No. 0 or 1 icing tubes (tips).

Straight stitches are piped directly along the ridges or pleats as they do not distort the lines of the smocking. Zig zag stitches are created by the pattern used when the ridges were pinched together. Working the embroidery on these involves piping small straight stitches over the points at which you have already pinched together the ridges or pleats. Several stitches may be piped close together if you want to emphasise this part of the design.

Pipe the embroidery horizontally across a complete panel, then begin the second row and complete that. By using this horizontal method you will be able to neaten the piping ends of the previous row as you work along the next.

MAKING A LONG OR CONTINUOUS BAND OF SMOCKING

When applying more than one panel of smocking side by side on the cake, set the pattern on the first panel and attach it to the cake. Roll the ridges in the second panel, trim and apply it to the cake, before setting the pattern, butting it up to the first panel. Lightly mark the line for the smocking, then set the pattern, picking up the 'stitches' from the first panel.

When a continuous band of smocking is applied around a cake it is important that the last panel that is cut is made up of an even number of ridges. The special roller has an even number of ridges so each full-width panel allows the ridges of paste to be pinched in pairs. When cutting the final panel to fit into the space on the side of the cake, count the number of ridges and cut the paste at the end of an even number.

FRILLED SMOCKING

A slightly more elaborate method may be used for finishing off the edges of the smocking. Follow the first three steps for rolling and trimming the sides of the smocking, then continue as shown (right) to make a delicate frilled edge on the smocking panels.

Frilled Smocking

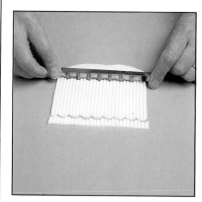

1 Use a cardboard template to cut the top and bottom edges with a straight scalloped cutter.

Finishing Surface Honeycomb or Chevron Smocking

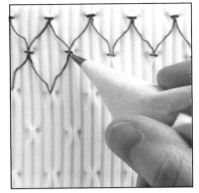

1 Working horizontally, pipe the embroidery along the first row where the pleats are pinched together.

2 Pipe threads from the centre of each stitch on the first row down to the pinched pleats on the second row to represent the loose embroidery thread lying on the fabric surface. Pipe a second row of short horizontal stitches over the ends of the previous row. Pipe more threads as before to the next row of pinched pleats.

3 The complete panel should be finished with a row of plain stitches piped over the pinched pleats.

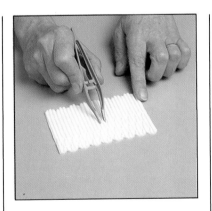

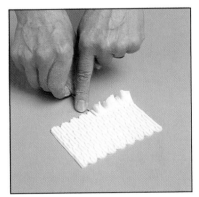

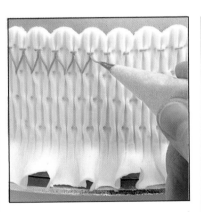

2 Set the pattern by gently squeezing pairs of ridges with the tweezers.

3 To frill the bottom edge, flatten out the ridges at the bottom of the smocking. Roll a cocktail stick (toothpick) across the edge to stretch and frill it out.

4 Attach the smocking panel to the cake and work the embroidery.

DESIGNS FOR CAKES

SUGAR MOBILE

The versatile sugar mobile makes an unusual party centrepiece for a variety of occasions. For Christmas use bright colours, bright ribbons and edible gum glitter. For a christening use delicate colours and fine satin baby ribbon. The foundation shape of the ball is made from modelling paste. Alternatively, this idea may be adapted to making cake balls. Use a spherical Christmas pudding mould to bake rich fruit cake mixture. Following the instructions for cutting sugarpaste and covering the sugar balls, cover the cakes in marzipan and paste. Instead of hanging the cakes they may be arranged on a board or displayed individually on a small stand.

500g (1 lb) modelling paste, see page 9
cornflour (cornstarch) or icing (confectioner's) sugar for rolling
a little royal icing, see page 8
about 250g (8 oz/½ lb) smocking paste for each ball, see page 9
food colouring

Equipment

smocking equipment
ball mould
flat piece of foam
1cm (½ in) wide ribbons

SMOCKED COVERING

Plan the pattern for decorating the balls before you begin to work on covering them with smocking paste. Either follow the designs illustrated on page 25 or work out your own design. The picture shows two balls covered completely in surface honeycomb pattern, using two different combinations of colours and small plunger cutter flowers. The third ball in the picture is decorated with a diagonal honeycomb design forming a 'V' shape on each panel. The same pattern decorates the top of each panel and piped flowers are added.

Use a piece of string to measure the circumference of the balls. Cut a rectangle of paper the same length as the circumference and the same depth as half the circumference. Fold the paper into four and use one rectangular section to make the template.

Mark the rectangle in half lengthways, then across in half to give four equal sections. Carefully draw in curves between the four points at the edge of the rectangle, as shown in the diagram, to create an oval shape. Cut out this oval template.

Roll the ridges or pleats, in a piece of smocking paste. Lay template lengthwise over the ridged paste and cut out the oval shape using a sharp knife. Moisten one ball with a little alcohol and stick the first oval section in place, with the points of the paste at the top and bottom of the ball.

Cut a second oval of ribbed paste, then attach it on the opposite side of the ball to the first section. Roll and cut two more sections and fill in gaps on the ball. Ease the paste together to close up and neaten the joins between panels.

Set required pattern with the tweezers, supporting the ball gently in the hand, then stand the ball on a piece of foam until coating has hardened. Cover the remaining balls in the same way.

Colour the royal icing as desired. Pipe embroidery in royal icing as far down the panels as possible. It is easier to pipe underneath the ball if it is hung from a bar and this also means that the embroidery can be finished with the minimum of handling. Allow the embroidery to dry.

Make large ribbon loops and tie them in place with short wires. Stick the loops into the top of the balls and secure with royal icing.

Note The balls may be suspended in a variety of ways; however a firm metal stand may be made. Curve three steel rods and set them into a block of wood which has three small holes bored into it. Cut a notch into the end of each rod to hold the ribbon. The base may be painted, covered with paper or covered with sugarpaste. The rods may either be chromium plated, sprayed with cellulose or covered with ribbon. A less elaborate stand may be made using metal coat hangers, twisted together for strength and wrapped with coloured ribbon.

Making the Template

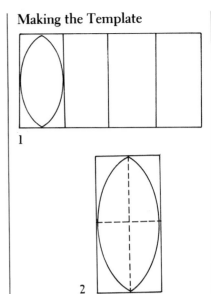

Making Sugar Balls

1 Roll modelling paste out about 5mm (¼ in) thick on a clean surface lightly dusted with cornflour (cornstarch).

2 Line two halves of a spherical mould with the paste, pressing it firmly and evenly into shape. Trim the edges neatly. Leave for 2–3 hours to set, then carefully remove the paste from the moulds and leave overnight to harden. Make three or four balls.

3 Stick the two halves of each ball together with royal icing. Pipe a thin line of icing around the edge of one half and press the second half firmly in place on top. Carefully clean away any excess royal icing. Leave the join until the icing has hardened.

4 Make a hole in each half using a fine metal skewer. Take care not to break the paste.

5 Thread a piece of ribbon through the top hole and out of the bottom. Use an upholstery needle or twist a piece of fine wire around the end of the ribbon to thread it easily.

6 Knot the ribbon at the base and secure it in place with royal icing. Allow the balls to dry thoroughly before applying the smocking panels.

Applying Smocking to the Balls

1 Use the template to cut a quarter section from the ribbed paste.

2 Moisten the ball with alcohol and apply the panel of paste to it.

3 Apply the second panel on the opposite side of the ball.

4 When all the panels of paste are applied, they should be butted together neatly so that the joins hardly show.

5 Stand the ball on a piece of foam and pipe on the embroidery.

6 Hang the ball safely, if possible, to finish piping the details on the bottom of the sphere.

Sugar Moulds

This mixture and method is suitable for making eggs, bells and sugar mice. If it is not possible to obtain eggs from a safe source and free from bacteria which may cause salmonella, water may be substituted but the finished moulds may not be as strong as those made from egg white.

1 Mix granulated sugar with a little egg white until it is the consistency of damp sand. Fill a clean mould with the sugar mixture.

2 Press down firmly, rather like making a sand castle.

3 Invert the mould onto a board and lift it off carefully. For a three-dimensional mould, make another identical shape. Leave until the outer surface is dry. Allow longer for a large mould as the walls need to be thicker for strength. Check after about an hour.

4 Gently scrape out the soft middle until the outside shell is the required thickness. Dry overnight (see note, right).

5 Stick the shapes together, if necessary, with a little royal icing, see page 5, and leave to set.

Note Hollow out the second piece and leave both to dry overnight until they are very firm and strong.

27

EASTER EGG

sugar egg, see page 27
food colouring
250g (8 oz/½ lb) smocking paste, see page 9
a little egg white, lightly whisked
a little royal icing, see page 8

Equipment

flat piece of foam
smocking equipment

Make sugar egg following the instructions for sugar moulds, see page 27. Plan the pattern for decorating the Easter egg before you begin to work on covering the sugar mould. Either follow the design illustrated or work out your own design. Knead yellow food colouring into the paste. The simplest method of covering a complicated shape such as an egg with paste is as follows. Roll out the smocking paste large enough to cover half the egg and the usual thickness. Using the ridged roller, roll the smocking paste from top to bottom. Brush the Easter egg lightly with egg white. Carefully lift the ridged paste, supporting it with a large rolling pin and lay it over one half of the egg. Take care to keep the ridges as straight as possible. Mould the paste around one half of the egg, working lightly to avoid flattening the ridges. Support the egg in one hand and trim the paste level with the seam all around the egg to give a neat line. Lay the egg on a piece of foam to cushion it before proceeding any further.

Using the tweezers, set the chosen pattern on the first half of the egg while the paste is still soft. The pattern used on the egg illustrated opposite is based on variations of the diamond stitch. From the top, the first border is made up of a half row of diamond pattern. The second row is an extended version of the diamond pattern forming deep 'v' shapes. The third row is a repeat of the first row. A row of easter chicks and flowers are piped to represent tapestry stitching, with a row of cable stitch below. Finally a diamond design is made up as for row two, then set again in reverse. Leave to dry for about an hour before covering the second side. This will ensure that the pattern is not damaged.

Continued on page 30

• Turn the egg over and cushion it on the foam. Repeat the process of covering as for the first side, making a neat cut to fit up against the edge of the first side. Set the pattern as before and neaten the join in the paste by gently rubbing it with a fingertip. Use a no. 0 tube (tip) to pipe embroidery on one side and allow it to dry thoroughly before turning over, then completing the piping on the second side.

Covering and Embroidering the Easter Egg

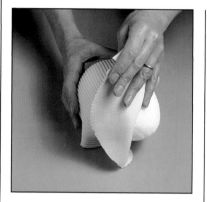

1 Gently mould the ribbed paste around half the Easter egg, taking care not to flatten the pleats.

2 Trim the edge off the paste around the join in the Easter egg.

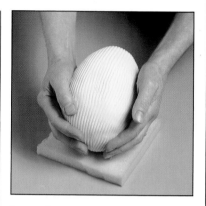

3 Lay the Easter egg, with ribbed side uppermost, on a piece of flat foam.

4 Set the pattern on the first side of the Easter egg while the paste is still soft. Leave to dry for about 1 hour.

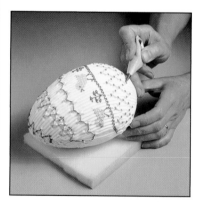

5 Cover and trim the second side, then set the pattern as before. Pipe the embroidery on one side; dry before piping on the second side.

SMOCKED BON-BON CASKETS

Gelatine paste is used to make the caskets which need to be strong. The caskets are covered with smocking paste. The working life of gelatine paste is only about 30 minutes, therefore all tools and templates must be assembled before the paste is exposed to the air. If any spare paste is replaced in an airtight container immediately, it can be re-used.

500g (1 lb) gelatine paste, see page 10
cornflour (cornstarch) for rolling out
smocking paste, see page 9
a little royal icing, see page 8

Equipment

smocking equipment

Draw templates as required for the bottom, sides and lid of each casket. Cut out these templates in thin card. Roll out the gelatine paste on a surface dusted with a little cornflour (cornstarch). Cut out paste shapes for the top, bottom and sides of the caskets using the templates as a guide.

RECTANGULAR BOX

For the rectangular box, allow all the pieces to dry. Assemble the casket by attaching the two side pieces to the base with a neat line of royal icing. Support these pieces until they are dry and set in place. Pipe royal icing along the base and sides of the shorter end pieces and stick them in place. Allow to dry.

CIRCULAR BOX

For the circular box, cut the top and bottom and allow them to dry until firm. Cut the sides in one strip. Pipe a circle of royal icing just within the edge of the base circle. Lift the side strip carefully to avoid stretching it and attach the long edge of the paste to the ring of icing. Adjust the shape to form a perfect circle. Pipe a neat line of icing across the join in the strip. Allow to dry.

Making and Covering Caskets

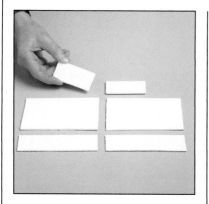

1 The pieces of gelatine paste should be cut out using the templates as a guide, then allowed to set hard.

2 Two sides of the rectangular casket are put in position and supported until the royal icing is hard.

3 The ends of the casket are put into position.
   Set the pattern in the panels of smocking paste, then apply them to the caskets.

APPLYING THE SMOCKING PASTE AND PIPING EMBROIDERY

Plan the pattern for decorating the casket before you begin to work on covering the moulds. Follow one of the designs illustrated on page 33 or work out your own design. Roll out smocking paste approximately 5mm (¼ in) thick. Use the special roller to roll the ridges or 'pleats' in the paste. Place template for the lid on the paste and cut around it with a sharp knife. Moisten the casket lid and lay the ribbed paste on top. Set the chosen pattern with the tweezers. The picture shows two caskets, both set with honeycomb smocking, see page 14. The oblong casket is completely covered with smocking; the round casket is set with diagonal strips of smocking, each three stitches wide, on the lid. This pattern is picked up by three-stitch wide panels of smocking around the side of the casket.

Cut ribbed smocking paste for the sides using the templates. Set the pattern. Attach long sides first on the rectangular box, then the ends.

Cover the circular box in a similar way. The side may be covered with two strips of paste and the join will be invisible as it will be hidden in between the grooves.

Pipe smocking embroidery over the lid and sides of the caskets. Pipe a neat row of dots around the edge of the lids and the edges of the caskets.

The caskets make pretty presentation boxes for sugared almonds or small bon-bons and chocolates.

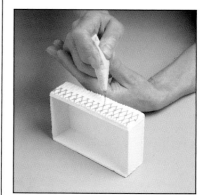

4 Pipe the embroidery onto the covered caskets.

BASKET OF STRAWBERRIES

1kg (2 lb) sugarpaste (rolled fondant), see page 8
food colouring
strawberry essence (flavoring)
oval Madeira cake, about 3.5cm (1½ in) deep, see page 13
about 3 tablespoons apricot jam, boiled and sieved
1 packet long thin chocolate sticks
a little royal icing, see page 8
500g (1 lb) modelling paste, see page 9
smocking paste, see page 9

Equipment

smocking equipment
no. 0 icing tube (tip)

The Madeira cake may be baked in an oval casserole dish if you do not have an oval cake tin. Brush cake all over with boiled sieved apricot jam. Cover the cake with sugarpaste, see page 17. Long thin chocolate sticks are used for the upright supports of the basket. Alternatively, roll long thin sausage shapes of modelling paste, cut them to about 7.5cm (3 in) long and leave to dry hard. Push an even number of upright supports into the top of the cake, spacing them out evenly around the edge. Set the supports in position with a little royal icing and leave to dry.

Colour some modelling paste or smocking paste cream or beige for the basketwork. Roll out thinly and cut into narrow even strips. Cut only a few strips at a time and weave each strip in and out of the upright supports, joining the ends of each one onto the next with a little water. Keep the rows of paste strips close together and continue to the top edge of the basket.

Make a handle by twisting together several strips of modelling paste to form a rope. Curve this into a 'C' shape on a board, making sure the ends are the same distance apart as the inside width of the basket. Allow the handle to dry hard before sticking into position and securing it in place with a little royal icing.

Cut out a template to the same depth as the basket, including the height of the cake and the weaving. Roll out a strip of smocking paste about 3mm (⅛ in) thick and use the special roller to roll the ridges, or pleats, into the paste. Use the template to trim strips of smocking paste. Set the honeycomb pattern in the paste using the tweezers, see page 14.

Creating the Basketwork and Handle

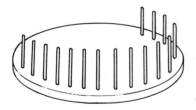

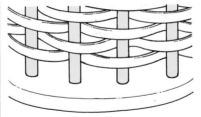

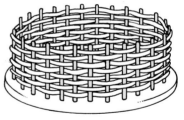

1 A shallow oval cake is covered with sugarpaste. Chocolate sticks are inserted around the top edge of the cake. The sticks are kept firmly in place with a little royal icing to form the upright supports for the basketwork.

2 Weave even, narrow strips of modelling paste between the chocolate sticks to represent basketwork. Join the ends of the strips together firmly by dampening them with a little water.

3 The completed basketwork should be even, quite firm and neat, particularly around the top edge.

4 Roll out three thin sausage shapes of modelling paste and twist them together to represent the handle.

5 Shape the handle on a board while still pliable. The space between the ends of the handle must fit the width of the basket. Leave until completely dry.

Make a narrow frill at the top edge of the paste and a wider one at the base, see page 20. Apply the completed panels to the outside of the basket. Butt the edges of the panels together carefully to conceal the joins in the smocking paste. Continue until the smocking paste forms a continuous band around the basket, measuring the final panel carefully.

Colour some royal icing red and pipe embroidery using no. 0 or 1 icing tube (tip). Use the remaining sugarpaste to mould strawberries. Colour a small piece green for the stalks; set aside. Colour the remaining portion of paste red and flavour it with strawberry essence. Mould small pieces of paste into strawberry shapes, mark the tiny indentations using a grater. Use a five-point calyx cutter to cut a double calyx for each of the strawberries from reserved green paste. Set aside to dry. Brush with edible glaze. Arrange the sugarpaste strawberries in the basket.

ICICLE CHRISTMAS CAKE

This design is suitable for a round cake of any size.

round cake, either Madeira or rich fruit cake, see pages 13 and 11
marzipan, see page 12
sugarpaste (rolled fondant), see pages 8 and 12
food colouring
250g (8 oz/½ lb) smocking paste, see page 9
a little royal icing, see page 8

Equipment

cake board, 7.5cm (3 in) larger than cake
smocking equipment
small pointed scissors
no. 2 piping tube (tip)
Christmas ornament or moulded decoration

Cover the cake with marzipan and sugarpaste, see page 16. Cover the cake board with red sugarpaste. Make a paper template the same length as the circumference of the cake and the same depth as the cake. Fold the paper in half lengthwise, then into three to give six equal sections. Wrap the template around the cake and prick through to the cake to mark each fold in the paper.

Roll out smocking paste. Using the special roller, roll the paste to make ridges or pleats. Trim the top and bottom edges using template as a guide. Set a diagonal panel of honeycomb smocking pattern, five stitches wide. Trim both sides of the panel. Snip down both long sides with small pointed scissors to form a fringe representing icicles.

Moisten the diagonal panel and apply it to cake centred on one of the points marked from the folds in the template. Make five more strips in exactly the same way. Apply all the panels to cake at the positions marked. When all the panels are applied to the sides of the cake they should form alternate plain and smocked diagonal stripes.

Colour a little royal icing red and a second portion green. Pipe the honeycomb pattern in two colours as shown on page 39. Using white icing, pipe a row of beads with a no. 2 icing tube (tip) around the base of the cake.

Roll out a long thin sausage shape of smocking paste, about 1cm (½ in) in diameter. Moisten a line around the top edge of the cake, level with the top of the smocking. Lay the strip of paste in place and press it

Decorating the Icicle Christmas Cake

1 Roll the ridges or pleats on the smocking paste. Set diagonal panels of smocking five stitches wide.

2 Trim the edges of the panels neatly and snip them to represent icicles before they are applied to the cake.

3 Roll out a sausage-shaped strip of paste and attach it to the top edge of the cake, then flatten it out to form a collar.

gently to secure it to the cake. Press the inner edge of the strip of paste flat against the cake with a modelling tool. Pinch the outer edge between your thumb and finger to flatten it and to make it stand out from the cake like a narrow collar. Snip the outer edge with small scissors to represent icicles. Stipple the top edge by using a sponge and dabbing on a little royal icing to represent snow. Pipe additional icicles under the 'collar' if necessary.

Using green and red royal icing, pipe small holly leaves and berries on the plain panels between the bands of smocking. Place a small festive ornament, or moulded decoration, on top of the cake and pipe on seasonal greetings.

4 Snip the outer edge of the collar and pull down bits of paste. Pipe extra 'icicles' onto the collar if necessary.

Two-tier Cake with Applique Leaves

28cm (11 in) and 18cm (7 in) round rich fruit cakes, see page 11
marzipan, see page 12
sugarpaste (rolled fondant), see pages 8 and 12
500g (1 lb) smocking paste, see page 9
food colouring
alcohol to moisten cakes
a little royal icing, see page 8
small quantity of flower modelling paste (commercial or home-made)

Equipment

36cm (14 in) and 25cm (10 in) cake boards
smocking equipment
no. 0 and 2 icing tubes (tips)
ivy cutter · 3 cake pillars

Cover the cakes with marzipan and sugarpaste. Cut two paper templates the same width as the depth of each cake and the length of the circumference of each. Fold each template into eight equal sections. Wrap the templates around the cakes and make a mark at the top and bottom of each fold, also prick a fine line on the cakes around the top of the templates.

Roll out smocking paste and roll the ridges or pleats into it using the special roller. Using the template as a guide, trim the top, bottom and sides with a sharp knife. Moisten the cake and apply the ridged panel, ensuring that the top edge rests on the guideline pricked on the cake. Transfer the marks made from the template folds to the smocking as you attach it to the cake. Set the diagonal honeycomb smocking pattern, see page 4, with the tweezers, starting each strip at a point marked with the template. Continue this process until you have a continuous band of ribbed paste all around the cake with eight diagonal bands of smocking. Using green royal icing and a no. 0 icing tube (tip), pipe smocking embroidery. Use a no. 2 tube (tip) and green icing to pipe a border around the base. Repeat on second cake.

Pipe pieces of lace on waxed paper and leave to dry. Colour the modelling paste green, roll it out and cut out leaves with a leaf cutter. Mark veins with a modelling tool or a veiner. Shape and leave to dry. Brush the leaves with dusting powders to introduce shading. Attach the leaves to the cake with a little royal icing. Attach the lace to top edges with a little royal icing.

VALENTINE HEART

20cm (8 in) heart-shaped Madeira cake, see page 13
about 3 tablespoons apricot jam, boiled and sieved
500g (1 lb) sugarpaste (rolled fondant), see page 8
500g (1 lb) smocking paste, see page 9
a little royal icing, see page 8

Equipment

20cm (8 in) heart-shaped cake board
carnation cutter
broiderie anglais cutter
smocking equipment · food colouring
no. 1 and 0 icing tube (tip)
sugar flowers or silk flowers

The cake should be about 5cm (2 in) deep. Trim the top edges into a curve to resemble a heart-shaped cushion, see page 48. Place the cake on the board and brush with jam. Roll out sugarpaste thinly, drape it over the rolling pin and carefully lift it over the cake. Mould the paste around the cake and trim the edges, tucking them under the cake.

To make the frill, roll out a small piece of smocking paste very thinly. Use the carnation cutter to cut out shapes, then cut each one in half. While working on a piece of paste it is essential to keep all the other pieces covered with cling film to prevent them drying out. Frill the scalloped edge of each section using a wooden cocktail stick (tooth-pick). Cut out the broiderie anglais pattern using the cutter. Moisten the straight edge of the small frilled sections and attach to the edge of the cake. Support with cotton wool balls until firm and dry.

Make a heart-shaped template using the tin as a guide but drawing the line 1cm (½ in) larger to allow for the curve of the cake. Roll out smocking paste to approximately 2.5mm (⅛ in) thick and roll with the special roller. Fit the roller into the grooves of the first section and roll again to make a large ridged area. Place the template on the paste and cut around it. Moisten the cake and lift the ridged paste over. Ease the paste into position; neaten the edges with a modelling tool.

Use the tweezers to set the surface honeycomb heart pattern on the cake. Use red royal icing and a no. 0 icing tube (tip) to pipe the embroidery. Use a no. 1 tube (tip) and white icing to pipe a border of dots around the pillow. Use white icing to pipe dots on the broiderie anglais frill. Arrange a spray of flowers in the middle of the cake.

SIMPLE PINK CAKE

18cm (7 in) round cake, either Madeira or rich fruit cake,
see pages 13 and 11
marzipan, see page 12
alcohol to moisten cake
625g (1¼ lb) sugarpaste (rolled fondant), see page 8
625g (1¼ lb) smocking paste, see page 9
food colouring
a little royal icing, see page 8
small flowers made with a plunger cutter

Equipment

smocking equipment
straight scalloped cutter
no. 0 and 1 icing tubes (tips)

Cover the cake with marzipan. Brush with a little alcohol, then cover with sugarpaste. Roll out smocking paste to 2.5mm (⅛ in) thick and roll it with the special roller to make the ridges. Trim the side edges with a sharp knife. Use a straight scalloped cutter to trim the top and bottom edges. Use the tweezers to set the surface honeycomb pattern.

Frill the bottom edge of the panel, see page 20. Moisten the side of the cake and apply the panel. Roll and trim more panels in the same way but do not set the pattern before applying them to the cake. The panels should form a continuous band around the cake. Count the ridges before cutting the last panel and cut after an even number, see page 20.

Colour royal icing pink and pipe the embroidery using a no. 0 tube (tip). Pipe the dots around the top edge of the cake using a no. 0 tube (tip). Attach small plunger flowers around the bottom of the cake, just above the frill, and arrange a spray of flowers on top of the cake.

A Christening Pillow

This delicate, unusual christening cake is made from a Madeira cake which should be baked to a depth of about 5cm (2 in).

20cm (8 in) square Madeira cake, see page 13
about 3 tablespoons apricot jam, boiled and sieved
750g (1½ lb) sugarpaste (rolled fondant), see page 8
500g (1 lb) smocking paste, see page 9
alcohol to moisten cake
a little royal icing, see page 8
food colouring

Equipment

smocking equipment
no. 0 and 1 icing tubes (tips)
0.9m (1 yd) 5mm (¼ in) wide ribbon, cut into 1.5cm (¾ in) lengths

Trim the cake into a pillow shape following the step-by-step diagrams, see page 48.

Brush one side of the cake with boiled sieved apricot jam and cover with a thin layer of sugarpaste. Trim the edges. Turn cake over and cover the other side in the same way. Trim the edges. Press the top and bottom edges of the cake together firmly to make a neat seam, enclosing the cake completely.

To make the frill, roll out a piece of smocking paste thinly. Using a frill cutter, cut out a 3.5cm (1½ in) wide strip. Roll a cocktail stick over the edge all along one long side to frill the paste, leaving a narrow straight strip about 1cm (½ in) wide, see page 20.

Moisten the plain edge of the frill and attach it to the underside of the pillow. Adjust the folds neatly. Support the frill with cotton wool balls to keep it in shape. Make more frilled strips and repeat until the pillow is surrounded by a frill.

The smocking design for this pillow is made up of a wide central panel of diamond pattern with narrow bands of surface honeycomb in a single line on either side. Either follow this design or plan an alternative pattern of your choice.

Roll out smocking paste until it is approximately 5mm (¼ in) thick. Roll the special roller firmly across the paste, forming deep ridges. Once you have rolled one strip, set the roller to follow the ridges on the end of the strip and roll the paste again to increase the width of the

Cutting the Cake

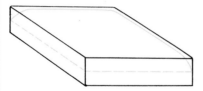

1 Trim off the square edges of a 20cm (8 in) square Madeira cake to create the shape of a rounded pillow.

2 Turn the cake over and trim off the square edges on the second side.

ridged area. When all the paste is neatly ribbed, measure and cut a 20cm (8 in) square. You will find it easier to cut out a 20cm (8 in) square of paper to use as a guide if you do not have a good eye for cutting straight lines.

Set the pattern making the central diamond pattern four diamonds wide. Set two, two-stitch wide panels of surface honeycomb on either side of the diamond panel. Brush the surface of the cake with alcohol to moisten it, then carefully lift the smocked square and place it centrally on the pillow. Make sure that all corners and edges are neatly matching. Colour the royal icing as desired and use a no. 0 icing tube (tip) to pipe the embroidery, following the picture on page 47 as a guide.

Make small evenly spaced cuts around the edge of the cake with a ribbon-insertion tool or a narrow-bladed kitchen knife. Insert the lengths of ribbon in the slits. Pipe a neat row of beading around the edge of the smocking with a no. 1 icing tube (tip). A picot edge may be added to the edge of the frill by piping a series of small dots on it. Use no. 0 tube (tip) to pipe fine lace pieces on waxed paper and leave to harden overnight. Attach the lace to the base of the frill by piping dots of icing to support and fix them.

Making and Attaching the Frill

1 Brush the first side of the cake with apricot jam and cover with sugarpaste. Trim the edge. Turn the cake over and repeat the process on the second side.

2 Press the edges together to seal in the cake.

3 Lengths of frill should measure 3.5cm (1½ in) wide and there should be a plain, 1cm (½ in) narrow edge of unfrilled paste within this.

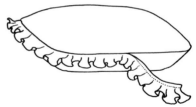

4 Attach the plain side of the frill to the underside of the pillow. Support the frill with cotton wool balls.

Petal Cake

This cake has six petals. Alternate petals are smocked and the frilled edge of the smocking is extended across the plain petals in between.

petal-shaped cake, either Madeira or rich fruit cake, see
pages 13 and 11
marzipan, see page 12
sugarpaste (rolled fondant), see pages 8 and 12
250g (8 oz/½ lb) smocking paste, see page 9
alcohol to moisten cake
food colouring
a little royal icing, see page 8

Equipment

straight scalloped cutter
smocking equipment
no. 0 or 1 and 1 or 2 icing tubes (tips)
sugar flowers or silk flowers

Cover the cake with marzipan and sugarpaste, as necessary, see page 16. Make a paper template to fit the side of one petal. Make a second template with the same dimensions but cut out a deep curve following the dotted line as shown in the diagram.

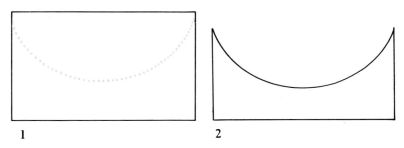

1   2

Roll out the smocking paste and use the special roller to roll the ridges or pleats into it. Use the rectangular template to trim the paste to size. Make two more panels of smocking using the same template. Cut the top with a straight scalloped cutter and frill the edge, see page 20. Set the diamond pattern with the tweezers, then apply the panels to alternate petals on the cake. Moisten the relevant section of cake with a little alcohol to ensure the smocking panels stick.

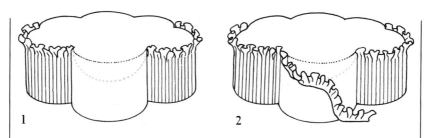

1   2

Use the curved template to mark the line for the frill on each of the plain petals. Use a pin to prick the shape of the curve on the cake. Use a piece of thread to measure the length of the curve, cutting it to the right length. Use this piece of thread to cut the frill to length. Make a narrow frill to the same width as the one at the top of the smocking. Dampen the plain edge and attach it to the cake, following the curve of pin pricks on one plain petal. The frilled edge should be standing upright as you apply it to the cake. Adjust the ends of the frill to meet the ends of the frill above the smocked panels. Arrange the folds of the frill neatly. Repeat on the remaining plain panels.

Colour the royal icing and use a no. 0 or 1 icing tube (tip) to pipe the embroidery on alternate panels. Pipe a fine embroidered border beneath the frill and at the side edges of the smocked panels. Use a no. 2 icing tube (tip) and white icing to pipe a border of beading around the base of the cake.

Place an arrangement of sugar flowers or delicate silk flowers on top of the cake.

ALTERNATIVE METHOD OF ATTACHING FRILL

This method should only be used when the cake has been covered for a few days and the icing is firm. Attach smocked panels to alternate petals as in the main recipe but leaving the top edge cut plain. Place a piece of perspex or a smooth cake board on top of the cake, then turn the cake upside down. Cut narrow sections of frill, flute one edge with a cocktail stick and attach to the cake, across the top of the smocking and following the curved guideline in between panels. Leave to set for a few minutes. Turn cake back to original position and adjust frills.

A SIMPLE CELEBRATION CAKE

This simple cake is surrounded with a band of frilled smocking. It is ideal for special birthdays, Mother's day or any anniversary.

18cm (7 in) round cake, either Madeira or rich fruit cake, see
pages 13 and 11
marzipan, see page 12
625g (1¼lb) sugarpaste (rolled fondant), see page 8
food colouring
500g (1 lb) smocking paste, see page 9
a little royal icing, see page 8

Equipment

smocking equipment
no. 0 or 1 icing tube (tip)
sugar flowers or silk flowers
1.5mm (¾ in) or 3mm (⅛ in) wide ribbons

Cover the cake with marzipan. Tint the sugarpaste with yellow food colouring and use to cover the cake, see page 16. Make a paper template 1cm (½ in) less than the depth of, and the same length as, the circumference of the cake. Use a pin to prick a fine guideline around the cake using the template as a guide.

Roll out the smocking paste. Use the special roller to roll ridges in the paste. Use the same template to trim the top and bottom of the paste. Trim the sides neatly. Frill the top and bottom edges of the paste, following instructions on page 20.

Apply the first panel of smocking to the cake, then set the honeycomb pattern with tweezers, keeping the lines straight. Make more panels and attach them to the cake to completely cover the side. Butt each panel up to the previous section to conceal the join. Neaten the frills as you go.

Colour some royal icing yellow and some brown. Use an icing tube (tip) no. 0 or 1 and pipe the embroidery on the smocking. Make a bow of ribbon with trailing ends and attach it to the cake with a little royal icing. Place a spray of sugar flowers or silk flowers on the top of the cake. Never stick wires into the cake and remove the spray before cutting the cake.

DELICATE MAUVE CAKE

This more elaborate cake combines a continuous band of smocking
with an inset panel of extension work to lighten the effect.

sugarpaste (rolled fondant), see pages 8 and 12
food colouring
round rich fruit cake, see page 11
marzipan, see page 12
500g (1 lb) smocking paste, see page 9
alcohol to moisten cake
a little royal icing, see page 8

Equipment

straight scalloped cutter
smocking equipment
no. 0, 1 or 2 and 00 icing tubes (tips)
circular frill cutter, see method

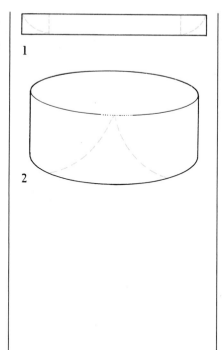

Tint the sugarpaste mauve with food colouring. Cover the cake with
marzipan and sugarpaste, see page 16. Cut a template the same length
as the circumference of the cake and 1cm (½ in) less than the depth of
the cake. Fold the template in half. Fold the cut ends over to mark the
desired width of the curve. Open the end flat again and draw a curve
from the top left corner to the bottom right of the mark as shown in
diagram 1. Cut the ends to the curved shape.

Place the template around the cake and mark the triangular inset as
shown in diagram 2. Roll out the smocking paste and use the special
roller to roll the ridges or pleats in a piece of smocking paste. Cut off the
sections with curved ends from the template and use these as a guide for
cutting two curved pieces of smocking. Cut the top edge of the
smocking with a straight scalloped cutter.

Moisten the cake with a little alcohol and attach one curved panel of
paste, following the guidelines marked on the cake. Repeat with the
second panel of paste, leaving a triangular shape in the middle. Use the
tweezers to set the honeycomb pattern in the sections of smocking
attached to the cake.

Cut more straight panels of smocking paste, roll the ridges into them,
trim and apply them to the cake, neatly butting all edges together. Each
piece must be made up of an even number of ridges. The cake sides
should be completely covered in smocking apart from the triangular

Applying the Smocking to the Cake

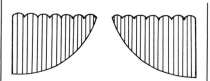

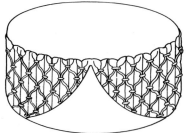

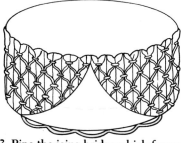

1 Use the template to cut curved ridged sections of smocking paste. Apply these to the cake following the guidelines marked.

2 Set the pattern in the curved sections when they are attached to cake. Set the pattern in the remaining panels when they are applied to the cake.

3 Pipe the icing bridge which forms the base for the extension work. Pipe the first row of extension work from the point marked out above.

shape. The last piece to be added must be cut to the exact size of the space on the cake and it must be made up of an even number of ridges. Set the pattern in each panel as before. Use a no. 0 icing tube (tip) and the royal icing to pipe the embroidery.

Work two rows of tiered extension work in the triangular space on the side of the cake. Pipe the bridges with a no. 1 or 2 icing tube (tip). Pipe the curtain work with a no. 0 or 00 icing tube (tip). Leave to dry.

Use smocking paste for the frill. Using a circular frill cutter with a very large centre hole make a narrow 1cm (½ in) frill. A 5cm (2 in) pastry cutter or the rim of a glass may be used to cut the centre out of the frill. Run a cocktail stick (toothpick) back and forth across the edge of the paste to frill it, see page 20. Attach the frill to the curved edge of the smocking, taking great care not to touch the extension work. Continue the frill all around the base of the cake.

Pipe a neat line of embroidery to conceal the line where the frill joins the cake. The smocking paste will set quickly and it will stand well away from the delicate extension work.

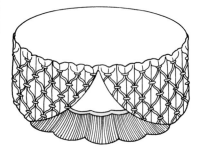

4 When the first row of extension-work is complete, pipe the bridge above it ready for another row of extension work.

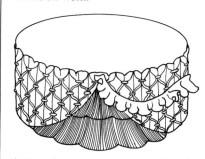

Note Instructions for piping the extension work are not included in this book as the technique is covered in detail in other general books on cake decorating.

5 Complete the extension work and allow it to dry before applying the frill. Begin by applying the frill along the curved edges of the smocking, then continue all around the base of the cake.

Pink Cake with Smocked Underskirt

round cake, either Madeira or rich fruit cake, see pages 13 and 11
marzipan, see page 12
sugarpaste (rolled fondant), see pages 8 and 12
food colouring
250g (8 oz/½ lb) smocking paste, see page 9
a little royal icing, see page 8

Equipment

straight scalloped cutter
smocking equipment
circular frill cutter
no. 1 and 0 or 00 icing tubes (tips)

Cover the cake with marzipan. Tint the sugarpaste pink and use to cover the cake. Make a template the same length as the circumference of the cake and the same depth as the cake. Divide the template into three equal sections. Fold the paper sections over each other and mark a double scallop through the paper. Mark the scallop in pencil, then prick it through the paper. Open out the template and make sure the scallop markings are clear on each section.

Wrap the template around cake and prick the scallop design very lightly through to the cake. Make a cardboard template for the area under the scallops: this is the area which is to be smocked.

Work the smocked areas first. Roll out the smocking paste and use the special roller to roll grooves in it. Use the template to cut out a triangular shape. Cut the bottom edge of the smocking panel with a straight scalloped cutter and frill it, see page 20. Using the tweezers, set the surface honeycomb pattern in the smocking. Apply the section to the cake, taking care not to allow it to extend above the curved guideline. Repeat until you have cut and applied all three sections of smocking. Roll a narrow strip of sugarpaste and make a 1cm (½ in) frill to fit between the panels of smocking around the base of the cake. Use a no. 0 icing tube (tip) and white royal icing to pipe the honeycomb embroidery on the smocking.

Use a no. 1 icing tube (tip) to pipe the bridgework for extension work, about twelve rows deep. When completely dry pipe the fine curtain-work using a no. 00 or 0 icing tube (tip). Pipe pieces of lace on waxed paper and leave them to dry overnight. Attach to top edge of the extension work.

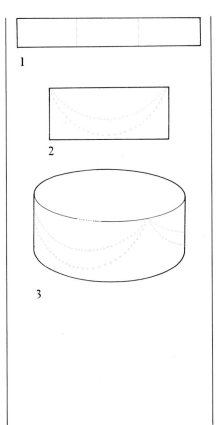

Applying the Smocking to the Cake

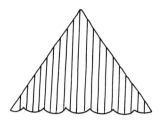

1 Cut the smocking paste into a triangle using the template as a guide. Trim the base with a straight scalloped cutter.

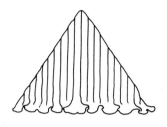

2 Frill the bottom edge of the smocking panel. Set the honeycomb pattern.

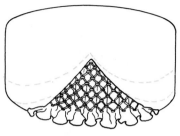

3 Position the triangle of smocking paste under the bottom guideline for the extension work.

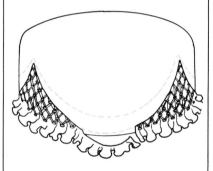

4 Add a narrow frill between sections of smocking.

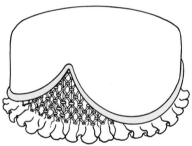

5 Pipe the bridgework on the bottom guideline.

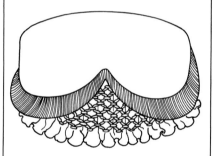

6 Pipe extension work from top guideline to the bridge.

THREE-TIER WEDDING CAKE

Narrow panels of smocking lighten the effect of the technique and the embroidery is coloured to tone well with the flowers. This design is suitable for cakes covered with sugarpaste or with royal icing.

25cm (10 in), 20cm (8 in) and 15cm (6 in) round rich fruit
cakes, see page 11
2.25kg (4½ lb) marzipan, see page 12
2.25kg (4½ lb) sugarpaste (rolled fondant), see page 8
icing (confectioner's) sugar for rolling out
500g (1 lb) smocking paste, see page 9
alcohol to moisten cakes
food colouring
a little royal icing, see page 8

Equipment

36cm (14 in), 25cm (10 in) and 20cm (8 in) cake boards
smocking equipment
moulded flowers or silk flowers

Cover the cakes with marzipan and sugarpaste. Make three templates 1cm (½ in) less in width than the depth of the cakes and the same length as the circumference of the cakes. Fold each template into six equal sections. One at a time, wrap the templates around the cakes and mark the cakes at the top and bottom of each crease on the templates, also prick a line around the top edges of the cakes following the line of the templates. Cut cardboard templates from one section of each of the original templates. These will vary in size slightly for each of the cakes.

Roll out the smocking paste. Using the special roller, roll the ridges, or pleats in the paste. As the panels on the sides of the cakes are quite small, a large piece of paste may be rib-rolled and several sections can be cut from it. Working on one cake, use the template of the panel to trim the paste. Set the surface honeycomb pattern. Moisten one panel on the cake with alcohol and apply the panel of smocking to it. Repeat until alternate sections on the side of the cake are covered with smocking. Use a curved modelling tool or the end of a teaspoon to flatten the top edge of the smocked panel, blending it onto the icing, to make it appear to be part of flat icing on the cake. Colour a little royal

icing pale yellow and use a no. 0 icing tube (tip) to pipe smocking embroidery. Pipe embroidery or dots to form a picot edge along the side edges of the smocked panels. This edging should disguise the joins in the paste. Pipe neat beading around the base of the cakes. Fix piped lace around the top edge of the cake, along the marked guideline, using a little white royal icing. Complete the other cakes in the same way.

Place the cakes on a stand, or assemble them using pillars, then add an arrangement of moulded flowers or silk flowers to the top cake.

INDEX

Published 1990 by Merehurst Limited,
Ferry House, 51–57 Lacy Road, Putney,
London, SW15 1PR

ISBN 1 85391 130 5

Edited by Bridget Jones
Designed by Bill Mason
Photography by Stewart Grant
Typeset by Rowland Phototypesetting Limited,
Bury St Edmunds, Suffolk
Colour separation by
Scantrans Pte, Limited, Singapore
Printed in Italy
by New Interlitho, SpA, Milan

The special smocking tools are available from sugarcraft retailers
throughout the British Isles. In the United States of America the
smocking tools are available from Parrish's Cake Decorating
Supplies Inc., 314 West 58th Street, Los Angeles, CA90037.
However, in case of difficulty in obtaining them, or for additional
information on overseas distribution, please contact Cynthia Venn,
3 Anker Lane, Stubbington, Fareham, Hants PO14 3HF.